GATHERING

GATHERING

SETTING THE NATURAL TABLE

KRISTEN CAISSIE

AND JESSICA HUNDLEY

WITH PHOTOGRAPHY BY

GEMMA & ANDREW INGALLS

New York · Paris · London · Milan

First published in the United States of America in 2020
by Rizzoli International Publications, Inc.
300 Park Avenue South
New York, NY 10010
www.rizzoliusa.com

Publisher: Charles Miers
Editor: Ellen Nidy
Design: Su Barber
Production Manager: Alyn Evans
Managing Editor: Lynn Scrabis
Texts: Jessica Hundley

Printed in China

2021 2022 2023 2024 / 10 9 8 7 6 5 4 3 2

ISBN: 978-0-8478-6370-9
Library of Congress Control Number: 2020951272

Visit us online:
Facebook.com/RizzoliNewYork
Twitter: @Rizzoli_Books
Instagram.com/RizzoliBooks
Pinterest.com/RizzoliBooks
Youtube.com/user/RizzoliNY
Issuu.com/Rizzoli

CONTENTS

8   *AN INVITATION by Kristen Caissie*

14   *MOON CANYON STUDIO DINNER*

26   *THE ART OF THE NAPKIN FOLD*

30   *LAYERS OF SPRING AT BOTANICA*

48   *FORAGING IN THE CITY*

64   *THE ART OF SOURCING LOCALLY*

70   *SUNSET AT FRONT PORCH FARM*

88   *LATE SUMMER SETTING IN SONOMA*

106 *THE ART OF SETTING WITH BUD VASES*

110 *THE POTTED TABLE AT BODEGA*

126 *FARMERS MARKET TO TABLE*

140 *THE ART OF THE GARLAND*

144 *OJAI CITRUS PICNIC*

156 *THE ART OF THE CENTERPIECE*

160 *BACKYARD BOTANICAL*

178 *EARLY SPRING AT THE OLD MILL*

190 *THE ART OF SETTING THE MOOD WITH CANDLES*

196 *A CALIFORNIA HOLIDAY AT HOME*

217 *ACKNOWLEDGMENTS*

218 *RESOURCES*

AN INVITATION

by Kristen Caissie

When life gets overwhelming, I try to find my way back to my original love of flowers. I look back at my nineteen-year-old self, working my first florist job, learning the names of various blooms, beginning to understand seasonality, discovering how to work with flowers and how to listen to them and how to tap into the intuitive process of arranging and design.

What has endured, in over two decades working in this industry, is that initial love. The flowers and my relationship with them is what really matters. This book is about that connection.

Growing up, it meant so much to me to be with family around one big table. Those childhood suppers, lunches and birthday parties are all alive in my memory. There were garden dinners by the late summer tomato vines and backyard Easter brunches heavy with the scent of lilacs.

When a table is set with intention, even the smallest occasion becomes a memorable one. When we eat outside, under the stars, or bring nature in, using botanical elements as décor, we elevate the day-to-day. And in connecting with the natural world, we also connect with each other.

Setting the table is a ritual. The materials we use (the heirloom plates, the thick linen napkins, the candlesticks created by a local artist we love) become part of the ancient practice of gathering, eating, sharing and healing together.

This book is my invitation to gather. It is my invitation to play and create, to drag your table out into your backyard and set it in a way that reflects the occasion, the season, the guests and the things you love.

*"FOR ME, SETTING A TABLE IS A SYMBOL OF
SHARING. AND SO IN THAT SAME SPIRIT,
I SHARE THIS BOOK WITH YOU."*

—*Kristen Caissie*

MOON CANYON
STUDIO DINNER

For our dinner in the studio, we gathered together the Moon Canyon team to celebrate and explore the range of what we could do together. My studio is where I feel the most comfortable being creative and where I have the time and space to really play.

For this table scape I was able to experiment in more of a controlled environment. As it was spring, I incorporated all of my favorite flowers, those delicate, early summer blooms.

Although this table may feel formal in some ways, I think it's important not to be too rigid or controlling. This arrangement is more heavily designed than some others, but I'm still bringing nature to the table, which means there should be an undercurrent of wildness, nothing too perfect or too ordered. I want to encourage people to explore their own ideas and not to feel like they have to rigidly adhere to the "rules" of setting a formal table or creating a formal centerpiece. Instead, feel free to experiment—by picking unexpected colors or using elements that aren't necessarily from the flower market, such as fruits, nuts or wild grasses. Setting a natural table means creating a moment that reflects the space you're in, the people gathered in it and how you feel in that moment.

I love styling with peaches and with other fruits and vegetables, as they add weight and a sculptural moment that offsets and enhances the delicacy of the florals. Here, I played with a variety of feminine, elegant summer blooms, such as foxglove, Queen Anne's lace and spiraled pea tendrils. I gave the centerpieces height and space, letting them run slightly wild out of the vase, as if they had grown there, sprouting directly up from the table top.

It all started with the peaches. These were special peaches, the colors of sunrise or a baby's cheek, but with a slight hint of green. These peaches became the inspiration for the entire table. They contained every shade reflected in the florals, the décor and the linens. This is a good way to start an arrangement, with one inspirational piece. I placed the peaches in small groups around the vases, so they felt casually strewn, making sure to allow for some wildness, nothing too orderly, but rather letting the flowers and fruits speak for themselves.

This arrangement marked the day I realized I loved lime green. While it's bold and demands attention, it also complements and offsets the flushed and fragile shades of the rest of table, the soft yellows, pale pinks and creams.

The table scape is a celebration of many of the collaborators I've worked with over the years. Our friends at Kalon lent us all the furniture. A Los Angeles-based design firm, Kalon creates modern, streamlined tables, stools, and chairs that retain a sensual, earthy feeling. For me, this particular table mirrored the core themes of this book. Setting the table is a ritual, laying down linen, placing the flatware and lighting the candles. I look at an open table as an invitation to set its surface in a way that best suits the occasion. For this arrangement we played with candle textures, mixing creamy hand-rolled beeswax tapers and smooth pillar candles from Creative Candles in a color they call Spring Green. The linens are vintage in a classic shade of ivory. We used Humble Ceramics plates to punctuate the space, allowing the heavy black and dark browns to ground the lightness and airiness of the florals.

Later our whole team sat down to eat together. Gemma and I made a pea, burrata and peach salad, we opened a few bottles of orange wine, and together we toasted our years of creative collaborations.

THE ART OF
THE NAPKIN FOLD

The ability to elevate a table scape can be found in the oft-overlooked art of the napkin fold.

If there is one element that can transform your table scape, it is the deceptively subtle multipurpose linen napkin. Even if you use the same dishes and flatware at every gathering, if you change up your napkins or even play with varied napkin folds, any gathering can be transformed into an elegant and special occasion.

One basic tip on harnessing the versatile power of the napkin: have a few different color options in your linen closet, so you can vary shades to complement the food, florals, setting and occasion. You can hand fold a napkin in a variety of ways and use a diverse range of materials to tie or shape linens, such as ribbons, floral elements, and napkin rings. See some of our favorite napkin folds on the following pages.

The Kerchief

Serving as the perfect canvas for a small bundle of dried or live florals, this fold lends itself to both formal and casual place settings.

INSIDER HINT: Taking a quick moment to iron the kerchief after it is folded will help to create crisp edges and sharper points.

The Band

There are occasions when the plateware is the star of a table and in these instances I love the simplicity of this fold. By simply wrapping the napkin around the dinner plate it is easy to create and allows your guests to experience the subtleties of the serving ware, be it a dish or a bowl, delicate porcelain or earthy, artistic ceramics.

INSIDER HINT: Depending on the size of your napkins and the desired width, this fold can be done in either thirds or quarters.

The Tuck

I love a bit of asymmetry in a place setting. Here, instead of shifting the salad plate to the side, which you will see throughout the book, the napkin is nestled under one side of the salad plate in a tuck fold. While it's not always necessary, you can style this setting with a menu or with an accent of florals, herbs or dried grass.

INSIDER HINT: The rectangular fold of the tuck is simply the band with an added fold on each end.

The Roll

A napkin ring provides the perfect opportunity to add another layer of artistry to your table. From carved wood or a buttery leather cuff to a more formal metal ring, a rolled napkin secured this way mimics the vertical lines of the flatware for a dash of table setting flair.

INSIDER HINT: Napkin rings don't need to be purchased; you can get creative and wrap your napkins with items you may already have at home—ribbon, scraps of fabric, or even a floral element from the garden.

*LAYERS OF SPRING
AT BOTANICA*

When I create arrangements, I work from a place where the style of the tabletop conveys an organic connection with the environment around it. I want my work to reflect not only the spirit of the gathering or celebration, but also the time of year and location. At Botanica we hosted a brunch directly inspired by the California spring that was blooming all around us.

Botanica is a wonderful restaurant and marketplace in the Silverlake neighborhood of Los Angeles. Emily Fiffer and Heather Sperling, the owners and chefs, are close friends and longtime collaborators of Moon Canyon. The two are accomplished food writers who penned stories on restaurants for nearly a decade before deciding to open their own.

Our work ethos and underlying business philosophies are very similar. They come to food with the intent of providing their customers with meals that are local, delicious, healthy and beautiful. Botanica's dishes are not only tasty, but also exquisitely presented. Although we work with flowers and they work with food, we are both trying to touch people through direct experiences with the natural world—botanical feasts fit for *all* the senses.

In Los Angeles, the spring comes on quietly, then blooms—seemingly overnight. The mud and rain make way for acid green grass which sprouts from every hillside and wildflowers that seem to suddenly appear everywhere. We worked with Botanica and a few other Moon Canyon collaborators to mirror this feeling of sudden abundance, of everything growing verdantly and all at once. We played with this concept not just in the centerpiece, which runs the entire length of the table and seems to almost emerge from it, but also with a playful overload of layered textiles.

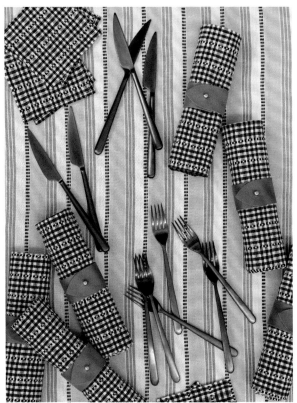

Heather Taylor Linens is a Moon Canyon friend and co-conspirator in all things beautiful. A Los Angeles-based designer, Heather makes beautiful linens for home and dining. She creates classic plaid and gingham textiles that feel ordered and clean no matter how much you layer them.

For our pattern-on-pattern tabletop, Heather Taylor's designs provide the perfect palette of colors and textures. We chose some of her traditional gingham patterns and layered them over a classic striped tablecloth. To keep a layering theme, we decided to use cloth cocktail napkins as drink coasters, keeping the tabletop linen-focused.

We placed the flatware and rolled linen table napkins, bound with pale leather rings. We custom made these napkin rings especially for our brunch at Botanica and Heather later integrated them into her own line. Then we stood back to see how else we could layer colors, textures and patterns.

Our many Heather Taylor linens were placed directly atop the graceful, clay-colored Humble ceramics plates. We went wild layering everything, wanting to make it feel nothing at all like a typical place setting. The colors were kept to a minimum, pale peach and storm cloud grey, in order to allow us to play more freely with pattern and texture.

So many of my favorite flowers are at their best in spring; lily of the valley, iris, ranunculus, and viburnum, to name a few. To create this spring garden-inspired garland centerpiece we used long and low metal vases filled with chicken wire and placed them close to one another. Then we layered in low, tightly packed greens to provide the structure to hold the taller, wispier blooms in place. In spring, flowers rule our world, so we thought they should rule the tabletop as well!

Botanica has an incredible menu of predominately plant-based dishes and an amazing selection of natural wines. For this brunch we had chilled orange wine with avocado toast on Bub and Grandma's delicious bread. We also had colorful crudité, put together beautifully—again, with a modern/maximalist approach.

Botanica created a colorful crudité board with an array of fresh seasonal vegetables. Seasonality is key here. There's nothing better than exploring the farmers market and being inspired by what's local and in season. I recommend talking with the market vendors about what's best that day and sampling to make sure the fruit and vegetables you buy are at their peak of freshness.

Boards like this are a simple, elegant way to provide delicious foods and eye-catching colors and textures. The best the season has to offer, creatively placed on your favorite tray or cutting board, can be an arrangement in itself, adding a unique style, décor, and pop of color to any table.

Don't feel limited to using only vegetables. Cheeses, dried fruits, nuts, fresh fruit, anything that tastes great and is easy to source (preferably at your local farmers market), can elevate a table scape while also satisfying hungry guests.

Here I did what I love to do by creating a wild runner that spans the entire length of the table. Spring is an amazing season to work with flowers as so much is blooming and in season at the markets. We envisioned a hedge of blooms, a wide, high spread that ultimately stretched to nearly four feet long. It's only one centerpiece, but it's got a lot going on! There's heuchera, which is a plant I buy often at the nursery to use the leaves and selected cuttings. Then there's popcorn viburnum, ranunculus, lily the valley, clematis vine. Nothing says spring to me like iris and ranunculus and lily of the valley.

We wanted the heavy texture in the blooms to play off the pattern-on-pattern theme of the linens. I could have even added a table runner to go on top of these other beautiful textiles, yet another layer to joyfully overload the barrage of stripes and checks and plaids. I'm not afraid of maximalist style, but I always try to balance it with a modern take. Here, the minimal colors within the textiles ground the wildness of the arrangement, which almost seems to be growing directly out of the table.

FORAGING IN THE CITY

Wandering through Elysian Park on the east side of Los Angeles is a beautiful way to spend any day of the year. But this past spring, following the long-awaited rains, the park suddenly became alive with blooms, the wild mustard growing taller than I'd ever seen it before.

Everything glowed a vibrant yellow as the flowers sprung up throughout my Echo Park neighborhood and Elysian Park, surrounding us with color. Every bloom swayed far above our heads. We felt like kids, the delicate mustard flowers floating up high against the sky.

I decided that I wanted to explore mustard as a floral story, one that to me is quintessentially Los Angeles. It's not the sprawl of pavement and freeway that most people associate with this place, but the overgrown bounty of the Los Angeles I know and love—the canyons, the coyotes, the swooping hawks and the magical places where the city turns abruptly wild, with nature taking over, as she always does.

The flowers I found and foraged dictated the colors of the arrangements. The point was to let go of the idea that flowers always have to come from the flower market. They can come from your yard, a willing neighbor's tree, you can find them blooming in the playground or along the side of the road. Just step outside, go for a walk and collect whatever you see. To explore what you can do with foraged flowers, I've created an entire arrangement using predominantly the grasses and florals growing just a few blocks from my front door.

I love wildflowers. You can do anything with them. Put them stem by stem into bud vases, or make wreaths or garlands out of them. No matter what you do they will be beautiful. Sure, they might not last long, but do they really have to? For me, creating with natural elements isn't dictated by their longevity. Many times clients will ask about their arrangements, wondering how long they are going to last. It's understandable, but it's not what enjoying or arranging flowers is really about. Each flower has a different life span and to me one of the most touching things about these wild blooms is their fragility. They're temporal and short-lived, but also incredibly lovely in the brief time they're here.

Gemma and I took a picnic out to the park for the day, bringing along a bottle of rosé and some sandwiches from our local market, Cookbook. We used our Nani Pani block print bandanas as napkins. Later, we foraged through the hills, gathering armloads of mustard and grasses for the arrangements.

I made the wreath on the following pages with mustard and nicotiana, which is almost like a tobacco leaf, as well as with Queen Anne's lace, dried grasses and a clematis vine that was growing in my yard. One of my favorite arrangements is to create a very simple ceramic-focused, vessel-focused table scape, as shown on the last page. Here, I pulled out my entire collection of D:Ceramics. Made by Denise Lopez, a Los Angeles-based artist, these pieces are inspired by modernist and Japanese pottery and have a warmly Zen, minimalist feel that both complements and showcases the freshly picked wildflowers and grasses.

You can just as easily begin a ceramics collection of your own. Be on the lookout for glasses, bud vases and bowls, collecting ones that catch your eye, whether they are created by artists you love or are thrift store finds or family hand-me-downs you loved as a child. Once you've amassed a few, pull your pieces out all at once and place foraged blooms in each one. Float flowers in the bowls. Create a wildflower centerpiece in a beloved vase. The point here is to not be too precious about it, but rather to do whatever feels and looks right at that moment.

THE ART OF
SOURCING LOCALLY

Some of the most rewarding aspects of being part of the floral and design industries are the relationships I've cultivated with farmers and growers.

Developing relationships with local growers has deepened my understanding and appreciation for plants and flowers. Beyond the general arc of the four seasons, I've become aware of how highly nuanced availability can be for a specific bloom. Reaching out to my local rose farm to source garden roses for an event may reveal that their cream roses aren't available due to a specific insect, or that last week's bit of spring chill delayed the expected blooms by another few weeks. Beyond attuning me more deeply to the seasons, the conversations and relationships with local growers have enabled me, in turn, to educate clients and friends along the way.

Using a unique bloom from a local farm makes a gathering feel special—it's an extra layer of consideration in line with knowing the provenance of the ingredients that make up your dinner.

There's something about seeing your materials in their original habitat, the garden or farm, that breathes inspiration into your design. Whether you're gathering blooms for one table setting or for a wedding, noticing the way the flowers interact with their surroundings or how they grow alongside other plants provides a wealth of ideas!

My designs always pay homage to nature. Texture, movement, shape and color are all informed by how I perceive the plants originally growing. I'm continually inspired by the real thing, by the nature all around me.

I've established relationships with flower farms while sourcing blooms for large events, but I've also developed close friendships with other florists with small cutting gardens of their own. In striving for the most beautiful florals and greenery, we've expanded our resources to include many local farms. I've shared some resources for farmers and growers I love in the appendix. Local farmers market are also a great source for seasonal blooms.

SUNSET AT
FRONT PORCH FARM

Front Porch Farms sits on a wild bend of the Russian River, a sleepy agrarian respite where the pace of life moves in rhythm with the rituals of traditional farming.

The land is owned and operated by longtime educators, conservationists and activists who have created a working farm and vineyard growing vegetables, grapes and flowers. Free of pesticides and chemicals, Front Porch's incredible floral harvests provide a bounty for flower fanatics from all over the state.

We happened to visit at the height of California's high summer. I like to call this time of year "Leo season" and use it as an excuse to celebrate my birthday throughout the month of August. Spending time with friends and family at Front Porch Farms was at the top of my birthday wish list. And happily, my wish came true.

We spent the whole day on the land, picking flowers and gathering vegetables and other ingredients for the food we would eat. Later, all the women who work at the farm joined us for dinner. These women live, work, sleep and eat on the farm. Every evening, after a day in the fields, they jump into the cool Russian River. Their lives follow the rhythms of the farm. To be able to be at this special place was deeply fulfilling for me. Everything moves slowly at Front Porch Farm. Time feels fuller. It was a beautiful Leo season day, spent out on the land and with the people I love.

The tabletop colors are a perfect reflection of the sunset golds and twilight blues that surrounded us in the orchard. I was inspired by what was growing on the farm at that very moment, the florals of the season, all the tones of the late summer crop. There were sunflowers of all kinds, as well as sunflower flocks, carrot flowers and zinnias.

Those August flowers have always had my heart. I had a bedroom as a child that for years was entirely decorated in sunflowers, everything from the bedspread to the dust ruffles and the curtains. I was surrounded by those shades—the vivid yellows, the strawberry blondes, the reds and chocolates. In a way they are *my* colors, the colors of my memories, of my early daydreaming, and of August, the month of my birth.

For the arrangements I wanted to create an idyllic, farmstead look. The centerpieces were verdant and overloaded and sensual, not too formal or fussy. I placed the flowers in simple ivory ceramic vases to let the flowers have the spotlight. We picked only what was at the farm, leaving the stems long and letting them sway and dip a bit, not trying to control their beautiful chaos. As we were hiking through the orchard earlier in the day, I'd found the loveliest apples on the ground. We picked them up and integrated them into the tabletop, scattering them across the stone-hued linen, letting them complement and enhance the centerpieces. We wanted the look and feel of the table to reflect the colors of the damp soil, the green fields and the orchard at its most verdant.

One of my favorite elements of this table scape was the absolutely stunning plateware, handmade and hand-painted by Ojai artist Rebekah Miles. I had commissioned it from Rebekah months before, asking that she include the blooms I knew would be in season. Rebekah creates ceramics that serve, in her words, "as functional paintings." Her work is delicate, highly detailed and utterly timeless. She creates modern pieces with a nostalgic, heirloom quality. These plates are made with a careful, thoughtful hand and are truly special, a sweet nod to both the flowers growing at Front Porch Farm and the favorite flowers from my childhood.

We brought a table straight out into the orchard, something I highly recommend everyone do as often as possible. Bring your inside table outside to your porch or yard or balcony; even bringing a blanket to the park will do. The point is to be in nature, to gather under a big sky with good friends.

As a nod to the farm itself we chose woven wicker chairs and laid down naturally-dyed gauze runners and napkins from our friends at Silk & Willow, along with simple silverware and hand-dipped, neutral colored candles.

We gathered in the late afternoon, the Moon Canyon team, my family and the women from the farm. The owners brought out what seemed to be an endless array of quintessential summertime dishes, almost all created from ingredients grown on the property—watermelon and tomato salad, fried chicken and a jaw-dropping homemade strawberry and rhubarb cobbler. There were also plenty of Front Porch Farm wines, plucked and pressed directly from the green vineyards that spread out into the hills around us.

As we watched the colors change, the day slipped into twilight. The blues turned to black and the stars lit up the sky like I've rarely seen it before, turning it into the darkest and also the brightest of nights. It was one of those moments where I looked around me and thought, "Yes. *Every* meal needs to be like this."

*LATE SUMMER SETTING
IN SONOMA*

Most of the vases I use to create my centerpieces are not very large. As a rule of thumb, I prefer floral arrangements to be two-thirds of the size of the vase. In this way the flowers take center stage. I often use chicken wire inside the vase to create a "nest" that allows me to arrange the florals without them falling out. As a base for the arrangements I used a long-stemmed tomato vine to create a natural "garden to table" feel.

Sonoma County's richly fertile Russian River valley is home to Shed, a farm to table collaborative that works with and supports the many farmers, wine makers and food producers of the region.

The realized dream project of founders Cindy Daniel and Doug Lipton, Shed is part community space, part market and part sustainable farm. The philosophy behind the project reflects many of my own thoughts on the role of the host and the importance of gathering people together.

For me, setting the table is part of a ritual that encourages intimacy, discussion and community. To focus on this concept, I invited family and friends to join me for a lunch I hosted at Shed. We came up to the valley for the weekend to celebrate "Leo season," as we call it. August (which just happens to be my birthday month!) is a highlight of California's subtle but distinctive seasons. And in Sonoma's northern wine country, the height of summer is, in a word, dreamy. The warm, sunny days give way to cool nights and the Russian River, running clear and clean, invites late afternoon swims while the world-class vintners of the region offer some of the most delicious wines you'll ever drink. I love to visit here during this season, escaping the dry desert heat of Los Angeles to enjoy Sonoma's amazing farmers markets, wander its redwood groves, explore its wineries and, of course, to eat.

For this setting I had the wonderful and all too rare opportunity to cut directly from the farm. In a sense, we 'cut our way up the coast,' clipping garden roses from Max Gil's beautiful garden in Berkeley and sourcing floral, wild malo and grasses from Shed's own plot in Healdsburg.

Cindy, the owner of Shed, arrived on the scene bearing a bounty of cut veggies and florals from her own private farm: chestnuts, roses, wild greens and herbs. Other florals came from our friends at Front Porch Farm, where we had had a magical dinner in the fields the night before. Almost everything on the table, from the flowers to the food, was sourced from mere miles away.

For the luncheon, a celebration of friends and family, I focused on creating a somewhat formal table setting, although I wanted to work with florals that aren't expected on a formal table, like shimmering dried grasses and curling tomato vines.

The most important thing for me was that the colors of the table reflect the multitude of shades of the farmland itself at this particular miraculous moment in the season. The interplay between light and dark is always key in my table settings, the ying and yang of varying tones. I get pleasure from playing with the unexpected, placing the silvery pale stalks of dried grasses alongside the more potent greens and crimsons of late summer vegetables.

We were so lucky to have Cindy and her chef at Shed create beautiful dishes for us using entirely locally sourced ingredients. I styled the buffet with risers to give height and dimension to the table scape and used simple but beautiful wooden cutting boards as trays. I also filled handwoven baskets with bounty from the garden and placed them throughout the buffet to evoke a sense of wild abundance.

The farm culture of the Sonoma area is undergoing a huge renaissance at the moment and Shed is an integral part of the movement. For this gathering, I wanted to create something that explored the agrarian elements of the area, creating a feel that's seasonal and also celebrates this very specific California time of year.

Summer in this part of the state offers a bounty of riches ready to take their starring turn on the table scape—freshly cut flowers and ripened fruit and vegetables, everything rich in color and scent. Taking these elements as inspiration, I set a table using the colors of the local farms, the shades of tomatoes ripe on the vine, of zucchini blossoms, corn and the dusty tones of the grassy hills beyond the dark dirt fields.

To me, the earthy, sharp scent of a tomato vine, of the leaves specifically, is simply the best smell in the whole world. I also love the evolving palette of a tomato as it ripens on its stalk, moving slowly from a bright flower to a green globe that transitions to yellow, orange and finally, to a vibrant red. So we used these changing colors as the foundation for our Shed luncheon garden to table floral arrangement.

All the tableware we use at Moon Canyon is meant to last. I hope that all your décor becomes an heirloom too. We love all kinds of plateware, so long as it feels special. We use everything from sourced vintage pieces to specially customized designs. I encourage you to work with local artisans and choose décor that speaks to you. For me, Humble Ceramics is that kind of plateware. Created by hand in the studio of Belgian-born, Los Angeles-based artist Delphine Lippens, these pieces have a clean, modern feel but are also subtly textured and somehow comforting in their heft and shape. I loved using the shadowy tones of the Humble ceramic plates as an accent color to our light and dusty "August in Sonoma" color palette. They lent a sense of earthiness and a groundedness to the setting, harmonizing the happy contrasts of our formal/casual, dark/pale, rose and tomato-inspired tabletop. I want people to think about how these elements come together, and how important it is to use décor you love, pieces you will have on your table for years to come and can pass down to the next generation.

The ritual of setting the table should always include celebrating yourself and your guests with settings that move you and make you happy.

THE ART OF
SETTING WITH BUD VASES

Bud vases are easy since they need only a few stems to fill them. I love to collect bud vases and use them all on one table, mixing sizes and shapes.

One of the most effortless table scapes to compose consists of freshly cut blooms set in a runner of bud vases. There's freedom to be found in this style of composition. Unlike a typical floral centerpiece, bud vases can mix and match florals, be sorted sort by color, or kept minimal.

Choosing a collection of vessels for this table scape is just as important as the blooms themselves. Here I used one style of vase that was consistent in its material, but varied in shape and size. This allowed me to mix and match the florals. If you're using assorted vessel materials or styles, you might want to consider keeping the types of blooms consistent in each vase.

Though bud vases do not require the arrangement techniques of a centerpiece, the placement, type of florals and vase selection in this simple table scape can feel just as impactful. You don't need a lot to fill a bud vase, which makes this the perfect design for clipping flowers and greenery from your garden. Just a few stems can go a long way and the negative space in the arrangements lets each bloom really be seen.

THE POTTED TABLE
AT BODEGA

Los Alamos is a sleepy, authentically Western town nestled in a golden stretch of valley between the farmlands of the San Joaquin and the Pacific Ocean.

It is located at the northern tip of California's Central Coast wine country and is currently experiencing a small but vibrant renaissance. Once a lonely stretch of road offering only a dusty saloon and a few boarded up storefronts, Los Alamos is now home to some of the best food and wine in the region.

Lately it's an area we've been visiting frequently, for weddings and events, many of them held at the newly renovated indoor-outdoor space, Bodega. We do a lot of weddings in the surrounding area of Santa Ynez and Los Olivos, so it's a place where we luckily get to spend a lot of time. Half the joy of traveling there is in the drive from Los Angeles up the California coast, which takes you past Santa Barbara and inland into yellow hills and ranchlands patchworked with grapevines.

Bodega is one of those places that makes you feel good as soon as you arrive. It's homey—inviting and elegant but unpretentious. You can settle in and relax. It is a place created for gathering together and celebrating, so it invites a happy, relaxed energy. A wine shop and tasting room, it also features a romantic outdoor space and a small classic greenhouse. Inspired by the latter, we decided it was the perfect spot to explore the types of table settings and table décor you can create entirely with potted plants.

A lot of the work that we do is with cut flowers, but for this setting I wanted to work with materials that last. Potted plants are a very easy way to decorate a table scape and afterward you can take the plants with you or give them as hostess gifts—they have the benefit of staying power and add a beautiful decorative touch to any table. Potted florals offer an enduring décor option for special occasions.

If you bring them home, simply put them on your patio table where they will live permanently as decorative pieces and provide longer-lasting enjoyment than cut flower arrangements. You can also add these potted accents to table settings, adding other floral details that complement the potted arrangements.

I'm a big fan of texture and of the variety that's found in meadow grasses and wild florals. I love how they each play a part, adding sculptural shape and geometry to a landscape. I wanted to play with that idea using potted accents planted with delicate grasses and petite florals. Wildflowers tend to be fragile and seasonal, but when I can I love to integrate them into table scapes.

For this arrangement we incorporated grasses like lamb's ear, Santa Barbara daisy, and yarrow. There's no focal flower in this table scape, just the planters themselves, which are decorative and spare. I wanted the pots for this table to be modern and clean, you can always replant the florals in different types of containers, depending on your personal taste.

*"YOU CAN EVOKE THE GARDEN IN
MANY WAYS, BY MOVING YOUR TABLE
OUTDOORS, OR BRINGING THE GARDEN
TO THE TABLE WITH THE CREATION
OF POTTED ARRANGEMENTS."*

—Kristen Caissie

Michelle Blade is an artist working in painting, sculpture, and ceramics. Each piece takes hours of work. Her process of etching and painting is deliberate and detailed and you can see this in the results. Her plates, which she custom-made for us, are keepsakes. These pieces are another example of the joy we get in working closely with and supporting other artists whenever possible. Sourcing tableware and other decorative items directly from individual creators and designers is a wonderful way to start a collection that is intimately your own.

For these pieces, I gave only a small amount direction, as I'm familiar with Michelle's designs. Her personal artwork often features elements of nature, so I mentioned I was looking for a summer setting and suggested that she integrate butterflies. She also added flowers and other dreamlike details in fragile, watery shades of blue. When the plates arrived I realized they could dictate the entire look and feel of the tabletop. I often work this way, when one item I particularly love inspires everything else.

The potting shed at Bodega is a beautiful structure, elegant in its simplicity. It called for a table setting that reflected the sparseness, earthiness, and the lines of whitewashed wood and glass windowpanes. We chose very classic linens, in stripes of blue and white, and thick ivory pillar candles that could hold their own among the pots. I selected glassware and silver for their sleek minimal design. I wanted the eye to focus on the delicate florals, sweeping grasses and of course, on the plates.

I wanted a table scape that felt cool, color-wise, mostly because we were so inspired by Michelle Blade's plates, which are white and a delicate eggshell blue, hand-painted, hand-etched and simply beautiful. We started with those colors and the feel of those pieces. From there we explored the idea of a potted table of early summer colors, whites and yellows and silvers—the shades of morning and twilight. The plates have an earthen quality to them, they are sensual and grounded and I thought they would be complemented by both the sturdy clay of the pots and the classic Belgian linens we used on the table.

We selected a few bottles from Bodega's stock from one of my favorite wineries in Sonoma. Run by fourth generation California farmers, Scribe makes beautiful, small batch boutique wines that are perfect for pretty much any occasion.

FARMERS MARKET
TO TABLE

At Bodega, a wine shop and outdoor tasting garden in Los Alamos, a tiny, picturesque village on the Central Coast, we explored two defiantly untraditional table settings.

Bodega itself defies expectations; it presents a new way to explore offerings from vineyards around the West Coast, all in a beautifully spare, modern space that feels less like a tasting room and more like a backyard party. Light-filled and elegantly casual, Bodega is nothing at all like the dark and stuffy wine cellars of the past.

In their sweet greenhouse and potting shed we experimented with a simple but statement-making potted plant setting. In their sun dappled courtyard, we played with another idea we've been dreaming about for a while now, a "farmers market to table" concept where we create arrangements using only elements found at the local farmers market.

For a long time we've been thinking of telling this kind of story with our table, of creating a design narrative all without flowers. There are so many ways you can decorate a table. You don't have to feel confined to one particular method—flowers in a vase, candles, everything formal and predictable. Instead, explore, experiment and play with colors and textures and shapes.

I started with the mushrooms, taking inspiration from their shapes and colors. Then I worked with some plants such as squash, cutting the stems and playing with the foliage to give it more dimension. What's nice about this type of décor is that it's so essentially seasonal. The most beautiful veggies at the farmers market are typically the ones that are in season right now.

Garlic scapes are the most beautiful little creatures. They have the most perfect spiral dancing look. And when they bloom they have such a pretty flower. We also used leeks, radishes and radicchio. Working with seasonal fruits and vegetables is an endlessly interesting way to set any type of table. I can envision a Christmas table set like this, using whatever you find in season in the winter months. For example, you could decorate with all kinds of squash or pumpkins—anything with unique shapes and colors that complement each other.

In terms of texture and sculptural elements, you can't go wrong with anything from nature. This makes my job pretty easy. There's currently a fascinating movement toward charcuterie runners, and using charcuterie as a centerpiece, which we've done for some of our events. We're not chefs, but it's a nice way to strike a balance between food and décor. And afterwards, you can eat it all! Grill one of those big yummy mushrooms. Make a radish stew and serve it with rhubarb pie and mulberries. What could be better than that?

This was our alternative take on a runner, or a garland. First see what's calling your name at the farmers market, what looks particularly good for the season, and then lay it down on the table. Natural materials have a way of looking perfect, even if they might not be exactly what you're used to seeing on a tabletop. If you trust your eye and stick with a complementary color palette, décorating with the unexpected can feel intentional, structured and not at all chaotic.

For this arrangement, we went with what drew our eye at the market and also with what we loved at the bakery. Bob's Well Bakery is an incredible spot in Los Alamos, just down the road from Bodega. If I could, I would decorate with bread all the time—it's wonderfully sculptural and the shading of the crust is intriguingly diverse. The bread and mushrooms set the tone of the color palette, all woodsy browns and grays. The radishes add an earthy pop of pale white. The garlic and squash leaves add a delicate green. These aren't plants I get to play with all the time, so it was nice to go to the market and gather items I simply thought were pretty and might go well together. You can do the same thing with citrus or melon or tropical fruit. I've done weddings where we decorated tables entirely with papayas and limes. We've done all kinds of food styling as table décor and it turns out beautifully.

For this table, since we were experimenting with the plants, we went with a muted, subtle décor. We left some of the veggies in the linen bags from Rough Linen we had brought to the farmers market, to add layers to the textiles, also from Rough Linen. We used natural, woven place mats, simple silverware and glasses. For plates we chose the classic "Rim Line" collection from Heath, the iconic California ceramics company. Founded by Edith and Brian Heath in 1948, Heath's aesthetic is earthy, elegant and timeless. We decided to give seed packets to the guests as hostess gifts, as a reminder of the "farmers market to table" setting and as a thank you for spending the day with us in this beautiful place.

THE ART OF
THE GARLAND

The lasting power of a garland makes it one of my favorite ways to design.

Garlands can be a great way to create a lasting table scape design that allows for a lot of flexibility. The versatility in size and shape of the bundles that compose the garland creates ample space for the placement of candles and food.

As far as technique, garland bundles are simpler than they seem. Here I used eucalyptus and dried grasses, layering and wrapping small clusters of each element, adding them together as I went. If you create a few different bundle sizes of varying fullnesses and lengths, you can use them on dining tables, buffets, mantels and other decorative spaces. I like to use a wrapped wire for my bundles, which looks intentional if seen, so their ends do not necessarily need to be hidden.

Garlands are a great way to showcase greenery and dried elements that could go unnoticed if florals were involved. If you use materials that dry well, what was once fresh becomes a piece that has aged, and will last longer, without losing its beauty.

OJAI CITRUS PICNIC

Ojai resonates with a century-old legacy of welcoming artists and free thinkers, offering sanctuary within the craggy mountain arms of this wide citrus-growing valley.

It remains a place for seekers, for those searching for both inspiration and respite. Nestled just a few miles inland from the famous surf breaks of Ventura County, Ojai is hidden by the Topatopa Mountains, and is shaded by towering eucalyptus, old oaks and groves of avocados, oranges and lemons. For Angelenos, it's the ultimate idyllic escape from the city, particularly in the early spring when the orchards are ripe with fruit and before the dry heat arrives. You can take farm or winery tours, swim in the cold creek or hike the endless trails etched into the rims of the hills.

We were lucky enough to be invited to a beautiful house at the height of the citrus season. Ojai has always been one of my favorite spots to visit with my family, so we packed for a picnic and all piled into the car. I'm not going to tell you that traveling with small children is easy, but I find it helps if the destination is a place as beautiful as Ojai and if there is the promise of a picnic. We are a family who picnics often. If we're going to the playground, I bring along a bag of food. For a car trip, we pack copious snacks. So when we decided to head to the orchards of Ojai, it was inevitable that we would picnic.

"WE LIKE TO EAT, AND WHEN WE CAN, WE LIKE TO EAT OUTSIDE. THE OTHER DAY MY SON SAID, 'WE'RE ALWAYS HAVING PICNICS.' FOR HIM, IT'S A SIMPLE FACT OF OUR LIVES TOGETHER."

—Kristen Caissie

I chose gardenia blooms and hellebore, and we plucked citrus blossoms to scatter across the table. I wanted the arrangement to feel casual. I chose lemons from the trees around us, gathering everything from the orchard in a big basket and bringing it directly to the table. I created the setting informally, letting the fruits and florals find their places intuitively, without overthinking it or trying to make it too formal or controlled.

For the arrangement we kept the colors simple and in a mood that reflected the yellows of the lemons, as well as the leafy greens and bark browns of the orchard and the pale rose golds of the mountains beyond. The sky was a clear blue as we gathered together between the rows of trees flush with fruit. We arrived early and set a sweet, unpretentious table for a breakfast picnic. We made fresh squeezed orange juice and I brought along biscuits and citrus marmalade. The kids helped me pick out some of the elements for the table, scooping up the beautiful lemons called "Pink Lemonade," which are true gems of the orchard, striped with green on the outside, and colored a delicate pink on the inside.

We kept the table setting simple, clean and earthy. The plates are from March SF, a store in San Francisco that is one of those amazing resources carrying exquisitely curated homeware. The glass and flatware are from the Los Angeles shop Nickey Kehoe and the tablecloth and napkins are from Rough Linen, which makes beautiful linens woven from European flax; their work has a timeless look and feel, making it the perfect match for a perfect day.

THE ART OF
THE CENTERPIECE

When thoughtfully designed, a centerpiece offers an eloquent expression of a particular place, moment and feeling.

When designing a floral centerpiece, I always like to have as much context as possible. For me any arrangement should reflect the purpose of the gathering, as well as the atmosphere of the space in which the event takes place. A great centerpiece tells a story, mirroring the underlying emotions of the occasion and pulling together the various elements of décor into a larger narrative whole.

This is one of the reasons why I often select specific and special blooms from local farms or make it a point to search the flower market for botanicals that have just come into season. Choosing seasonal blooms that are only briefly available allows for the unexpected and highlights the ephemeral nature of the gathering itself.

Some questions to consider when creating a centerpiece yourself or collaborating with a florist:

LOCATION

What is the venue for the gathering? Is it indoors? Outdoors? Where will the centerpiece live?

COLOR PALETTE

Are you working within a specific color palette for the gathering? Do you want the floral elements to highlight this color palette or do you envision a muted centerpiece to allow the other décor elements to shine on their own?

THEME

Is there an overarching theme for the occasion that the florals should echo?

What words come to mind to describe the aesthetic you hope for at your gathering?

OTHER DÉCOR ELEMENTS

What else will be present on the table? Are there specific plates, glassware, and tableware that you're using?

LOGISTICS

How many tables or spaces are you highlighting? What is the size of the table and of the space?

SPECIAL REQUESTS

Are there particular florals that you'd love to see in your centerpiece? Any that you would prefer to not see?

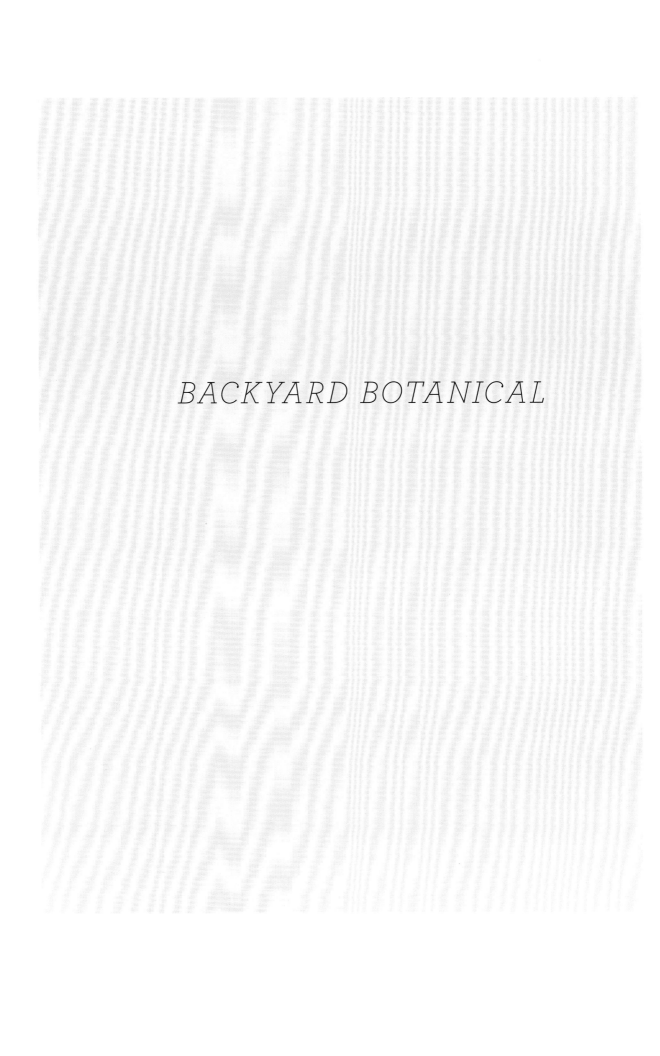

BACKYARD BOTANICAL

My friend Emily is an essential part of the Moon Canyon team, an accomplished gardener with a backyard continually bursting with seasonal flowers.

She is also a fellow New Englander and brings a bit of that East Coast sensibility to her garden and home in Pasadena. For this setting we created something more intimate, a gathering to celebrate the season's florals and plants while sharing a simple meal that reminded us both of our childhood summers on the Atlantic Ocean.

For our dinner together, I wanted to explore a botanical feeling, using vines and leaves to create a centerpiece that felt formal yet unique. Much of what we incorporated into the arrangements we clipped directly from Emily's garden, spending most of the day digging in the dirt and experimenting with different cuttings and compositions.

Later in the afternoon we laid the table together and sat down for steamed clams and cold prosecco. While it was just the two of us, the table scape we created was decadent and inspired, transforming the afternoon into an unforgettable, truly special experience. This is something particularly important to me, taking even a small amount of time to set a table and create florals with intent, even if the occasion is as simple as meeting up with a friend. For me setting the table is about ritual. Not only is the experience of arranging a table scape meditative and creatively rewarding, it also elevates day-to-day gatherings into moments you'll remember for a long time to come.

Much of the centerpiece arrangement was made from Emily's garden clippings and from elements I bought at my local nursery, which is something I do often. There are moments when I forgo the flower market, seeking inspiration instead at the nursery with its wide selection of living plants. I choose the ones that catch my eye because of their particular color or bloom, or the shape and size of their leaves. I use both the foliage and the flowers in my arrangements. It's always stimulating working with new materials and working with plants is different from the more traditional florals I use for weddings and events.

For these settings, I wanted to incorporate all kinds of botanical plants. We used jasmine vine, which was in season, raspberry vines, wild fern, columbine and hellebore. I supplemented these with cuttings from Emily's garden, making what appears to be a very traditional formal centerpiece, but out of untraditional plants. I placed taper candles inside the arrangement, which is something that I like to do these days, as it speaks to the ephemeral nature of floral arrangements. The flowers move through their cycles as the candles flicker, melt and are finally extinguished.

Since we were creating a botanical rather than a floral-focused centerpiece, we gathered items that felt complementary, like these plates with nature-themed illustrations from John Derian, who specializes in decoupage techniques. A collaboration between Derian and the ceramist Astier de Villatte, they feature intricate illustrations on a background of earthy white clay. We kept the linens classic with simple flax-colored pieces from the Los Angeles home design company Parachute. We used Emily's own vintage wedding silver and flatware.

As an homage to our memories of New England summers, we rinsed piles of fresh clams in Emily's garden sink and steamed them with garlic, shallots and white wine. We toasted thick slices of bread from our favorite local baker, Bub and Grandma's, and washed it all down with a chilled prosecco. It was a simple and delicious meal, shared outside in a beautiful place with a good friend. What better reason could you want for setting an elegant and considered table?

EARLY SPRING
AT THE OLD MILL

Pasadena is a place close to my heart. With its century-old Craftsmans and the orderly brick facades of its town center, Pasadena reminds me of the places where I grew up on the East Coast.

The stoic timeworn feel of its architecture is reminiscent of my New England home. While Los Angeles gleams with glass, sunblasted stucco and palm trees, Pasadena is weathered wood shaded by ancient oaks. The weight of history is felt in its structures, particularly in a two hundred-year-old grist mill built for one of the first missions in the San Gabriel Valley. El Molino Viejo, as it is called, is in fact the oldest commercial building in Southern California, an adobe wonder surrounded by formal gardens and bubbling fountains. Today, the original mill functions as a museum and private event space—the perfect spot to host a late winter gathering.

Winter in Los Angeles is rainy, misty and colder than you might think. But as the storms gently subside, the first bursts of green growth, a spread of verdant color, appear almost overnight. Late winter and early spring are beautiful moments here, the shades of the landscape are subdued, the light soft and dreamlike. When I was thinking about where to host a dinner during this brief but lovely season, Emily of our Moon Canyon team suggested the Old Mill. Emily belongs to the garden society that runs the space and takes care of its upkeep. I leapt at the opportunity, as the Old Mill is a hidden gem that I had long been wanting to explore.

We created a formal, slightly wild centerpiece using one of our favorite designs, an abundance of flowers and fruit that spreads nearly the length of the table and seems to sprout from the clay-hued tablecloth. Much of the arrangement was cut from the Old Mill gardens and Emily's own nearby backyard flower bed.

We played with textures, placing herbs and greens alongside graceful, traditional florals and adding in sculptural elements, like branches of geranium, citrus and silvery olive.

Later we made a tisane from some of the botanical elements of the tabletops—flavored with hints of calendula, mint and geranium. We incorporated the unexpected, passion fruit, citrus, and a spread of vines to mirror the ancient roses clinging to the garden walls.

We went to the farmers market for the citrus—these pops of color echo the yellow roses and rusty shades of the walls, the courtyard paving stones, and the plateware.

The garden walls of the Old Mill are made of crumbling grey stone and faded red adobe clay, a spread of earth tones interrupted only by meandering rivers of green moss that have found their way through the centuries-old cracks. The deep sea color of the moss was our primary inspiration and we set a table with hues echoing this underlying palette—emerald and jade textiles from the local linen company Matteo and plates in the same shade by the iconic California ceramics design firm Heath. We created a layering effect, a feel of sensuous, watery depths, with olive-hued linen napkins and place mats over a neutral, pale flax tablecloth. The pewter flatware, in a nod to the history of our surroundings, reflects the colors of the walls' ragged mortar and the courtyard's smooth, worn paving stones.

We laid a spread of cheeses and olives and lit the creamy candles as the sun faded behind clouds. Gemma made her homemade flatbread crackers and we sat around the table together, enjoying the last of the wet, cool afternoons, that brief, poetic moment of green and growth that marks a California winter.

THE ART OF
SETTING THE MOOD
WITH CANDLES

*Lighting is everything. An essential consideration for any
gathering, the choice of lighting plays a key role in evoking
emotion, creating a mood and elevating the atmosphere.*

The warm and flickering glow of candlelight is one of our favorite ways
to create not only ambience but to enhance the look of the tabletop and
surrounding florals and décor.

　　When deciding on the style and color of candle, as well as vessel and
holder, it's helpful to take into account the story you want your gathering to
tell. Where is the event taking place? Is it a more formal occasion? Or more
playful? Indoors or outdoors? All of these factors ultimately play a role in the
selection of candles and holders.

　　In this instance, we opted for a soft ceramic holder by Floral Society
in a neutral shade. The pale color of the base allows the bold colors of the
taper candles to pop against the table, while the shades of the taper candles
themselves spotlight the vibrant tones of the marigold heads. The variety in
height of both candles and holders creates instant depth, adds visual interest
and keeps the eye moving along the entire length of the table.

Some of our considerations when selecting candles for our gatherings:

For a more formal occasion, consider keeping the candleholder traditional, but bringing in a light-toned or putty-colored candle to add a hint of warmth and modernity.

While I love placing candles on the table without glass when the venue permits, for outdoor occasions, consider including a glass shield or a hurricane glass to protect the candle's flame and ensure that the wind won't take away from the ambiance.

For a long, rectangular table, consider using various sized pillar candles on platters and placing on the table alongside them loose blooms or greenery and vines. This is a simple, non-floral design that adds a touch of wildness and romance to any tabletop.

There are so many ceramists making beautiful taper or votive candleholders that feel like pieces of art. These pieces stand alone, without the candle, as their own decorative objects. It is exactly this type of thoughtful, collectible work that I love to bring into my home. You can display them as is or use them as intended. Either way, the beauty of the piece shines through.

A CALIFORNIA HOLIDAY
AT HOME

I grew up in New England, a place that forms many people's idealized version of the holidays, a tinsel and twinkling light vision of evergreens bent heavy with snow.

The reality of course, is different. I don't miss scraping blackened ice from my car's windshield, or the endless months of bone-chilling cold. And Los Angeles holds its own charms during the holiday season.

The rains arrive in the winter months and with them a cozy, contemplative feeling. It's a time to entertain inside, to bake, sip tea, build a fire and bring family and friends together around the table. For the holidays this year, I hosted a get-together in our home. My husband is a skilled carpenter and his passion and patience for intricate handiwork is formidable. He spent nearly a decade tearing out our home's old interior walls and crafting a light-filled living space detailed entirely with fine wood elements. I took inspiration from these warm, natural colors, the tones and details of our home, for these celebratory holiday table scapes and arrangements.

Our home's wooden interior and the flash of green from the bamboo outside our windows provided the core inspiration for my holiday décor. I built on these two earthy tones, exploring shades of ivory and cream, evergreen and jade. The dining and coffee tables, in a shade of wood that complements our walls and floors, were borrowed from our friends at the wonderful design house Nickey Kehoe. The softly rippled plateware, in a shade of damp snow, is from Guild, Roman and Williams's New York shop. We used minimal linens in the lightest peach to allow the natural wood of the tables to take the stage. For the dining table scape we added sugared rosemary sprigs for a hint of green and pops of seasonal yellow citrus. For the coffee table, I scattered sugar pinecones among various dried herbs and pods.

Winter here in California is the moment when things are just starting to grow. Outside, the colors of nature are predominately those of dryness, in shades of straw and husk, but there is also the first wave of growth dressed in brilliant greens. I mirrored this juxtaposition in the centerpiece, a mix of wintery emeralds with gold grasses and dried florals that I'd saved from the summer and fall.

For our holiday celebration, we created a traditional centerpiece arrangement, a loosely scattered garland and wreath. The garland was particularly easy, as I simply laid pieces down and arranged them in a way that felt right. No wires, no glue. This is how I like to decorate for the holidays. Don't overthink, don't overcomplicate. In the end, you can always simply put a fresh pine bough on the door and call it a day! I love working with dried botanicals in this season as well, they're long-lasting and the colors are subtle and refined. For these arrangements I used dried thistles, poppy pods, cedar and Victorian birch, as well as wild grasses and delicate beads of dried amaranth. I also added in eucalyptus that had been bleached, turning the leaves a fragile shade of silver.

For the holidays, I wanted to create menus and arrangements that felt connected to my family and home life. Much of the work I do is manifesting other people's visions, their expressions of themselves. But here I wanted to reflect my own tastes, as well as the colors that complement the warm, golden shade of wood my husband chose for the interior of our home. It is a color I love, a hue that saturates my day-to-day.

Olive Oil Cake

One of my oldest and best friends, Christopher Lier, just happens to be one of the best pastry chefs in Los Angeles. Christopher and his wife, Amy, joined us for our holiday gathering. We made eggnog with candied citrus slices for the occasion. Later, we cracked walnuts to snack on while Christopher baked one of his elegant and delicious cakes. He kindly offered his recipe. We hope you enjoy!

INGREDIENTS

150g whole grain Sonora flour

120g cake flour

   (or all-purpose flour)

1 teaspoon baking powder

1½ teaspoons kosher salt

3 eggs

330g sugar

1½ cups olive oil

1½ cups milk

lemon or orange zest to taste

PREPARATION

1. *Preheat oven to 350 degrees.*

2. *Place Sonora flour into a bowl and sift in the cake flour and baking powder. Add salt. In a large bowl, whisk the eggs. Add the sugar and zest and whisk once more. While whisking continuously, add the olive oil in a steady stream until emulsified, then slowly drizzle in the milk. Fold in the dry ingredients until well blended.*

3. *Evenly divide the batter into whatever molds you wish (first brushing the insides with a bit of olive oil to avoid sticking) and bake until a skewer comes out clean when inserted into the middle of the cake.*

I was introduced to this recipe while working at Nancy Silverton's restaurant Osteria Mozza under pastry chef Dhalia Narvaez. I'm not sure if it's Nancy's or Dhalia's recipe, but either way it's delicious! At the restaurant it was served in little two-bite tea cake sized portions with olive oil, gelato and pulled rosemary sugar. But it's a versatile cake that can be made in a number of ways: thinly layered with buttercream; or, due to the large amount of olive oil in the batter, it can be grilled for a crispy, charred exterior and a wonderfully moist, soft interior. I often like to make a mini bundt version with a lemon mousse in the center, or simply the way it's presented here, in a large bundt cake format with lemon glaze to finish. It's an easy cake to mix and bake, but has a serious decadence to it. You can use any olive oil, but the better the oil the better the cake. — *Christopher Lier*

Acknowledgments

This book wouldn't have been possible without the love, support and generosity of so many people. First, I'd like to thank my husband, Ryan, for being the kind of man who can support and love with great openness, allowing creativity to thrive. For the endless nights you heal space for me to discover myself in this process, I love you.

I'd like to thank Gemma and Andy Ingalls for coming along on this adventure with us. You've both been so generous with your time and craft. Thank you from the bottom of my heart for capturing this story.

Thank you also to Jessica Hundley for being my rock and my voice. I love you, sis. Your contribution to the story within these pages is immeasurable.

Thank you to our editor, Ellen Nidy, for believing in this book. To Su Barber for shaping the book, your talents and eye have created the world for our images to live in and it's beautiful! To Brandy Curry and Emily Day and your unwavering devotion to the dream. I love you, you make my world go 'round. To my ladies of the river, Katie Chirgotis, Elise Metzger, and Brita Olsen, thank you for coming along and contributing so much love to our Nor Cal adventure.

To all of those who have contributed their time, space, or art to this project, *you* have made this book what it is. Thank you to the makers whose tables, dishes, linens and candles provided me with the beautiful objects to express myself.

Thanks also goes out to:

Nickey Kehoe for so much inspiration and generosity.

Amy Lipnis and Christopher Lier, whose generosity and friendship are unparalleled.

Jennifer Medley and Fabrice Peno for providing space for us at their Ojai sanctuary.

Kalon Studio, whose beautiful craftsmanship is what table dreams are made of.

Rebekah Miles, you, my friend, are a true artist and the plates you created for us will live on in these pages as a testament to your love of your craft.

Michelle Blade, whose stunning artwork helped set the table and stole our hearts.

Heather Taylor, love you, sis! A forever collaborator.

Botanica Restaurant, we thank you for providing space, inspiration, and the yummy food for our shoot together.

Creative Candles we adore you!

Matteo Linen

Rough Linen

Heath Ceramics

Bodega Los Olivos

Front Porch Farm, your generosity of time, space, and flowers made my birthday dinner the most epic sunset evening ever.

Cindy Daniel at Shed, who contributed her space and food for us to co-create something so inspiring.

Thank you:

Floral Society, Old Mill Pasadena, Bluma Floral Farm

RESOURCES

*Following is a list of my top go-tos when looking for inspiration.
Whether it's linens, candles or dishes, all the essentials for
setting a beautiful table can be found here.*

Home Décor

Nickey Kehoe
Los Angeles, CA
https://nickeykehoe.com/

dekor
Los Angeles, CA
http://www.dekorla.com/

RW Guild
New York, NY
https://rwguild.com/

March SF
San Francisco, CA
https://marchsf.com/

Tortoise General Store
Venice, CA
https://shop.tortoisegeneralstore.com/

Shop Terrain
Nationwide
https://www.shopterrain.com

Lawson and Fenning
Lawsonfenning.com

Linens

Heather Taylor Home
Los Angeles, CA
https://heathertaylorhome.com/

August
https://augustlinen.com/

Matteo
Los Angeles, CA
https://matteola.com

Rough Linen
California
https://www.roughlinen.com

Les Indiennes
Hudson, NY
www.lesindiennes.com

Studio Ford
Los Angeles, CA
www.studio-ford.com

Candles

Mole Hollow
Western Massachusetts
https://molehollowcandles.com/

Creative Candles
Kentucky
https://creativecandles.com

Northern Lights
Wellsville, NY
https://northernlightscandles.com

Ester and Erik
Denmark
http://www.ester-erik.dk

Floral Society
https://www.thefloralsociety.com/

Ceramics

Rebekah Miles
Ojai, CA
https://www.rebekahmiles.com/

Notary Ceramics
Portland, OR
www.notaryceramics.com

Heath Ceramics
California
https://www.heathceramics.com/

Mt. Washington Pottery
Los Angeles, CA
http://www.mtwashingtonpottery.com/

East Fork
Ashville, NC
https://eastfork.com/

Humble Ceramics
Los Angeles, CA
www.humbleceramicswholesale.com

Simone Bodmer-Turner
New York, NY
www.simonebodmerturner.com

Henry Street Studio
Kingston, NY
www.henrystreetstudio.com

Wood Woven
UK
https://www.woodwoven.com/

Flower Farms

Front Porch Farm
Healdsburg, Ca
https://fpfarm.com/

Bluma Farm
Oakland, CA
http://blumaflowerfarm.com/

Sunny Meadows Flower Farm
Columbus, Ohio
https://www.sunnymeadowsflowerfarm.com/

3 Porch Farm
Georgia
http://3porchfarm.com/

Floral Reserve
Rhode Island
https://www.thefloralreserve.com/

Mayesh Wholesale
Nationwide
https://www.mayesh.com/

Blue Heron Farm
Watsonville, CA
http://blueheron.farm/

>